A GUIDE TO ASSESSMENT
FOR PSYCHOANALYTIC
PSYCHOTHERAPISTS

A GUIDE TO ASSESSMENT FOR PSYCHOANALYTIC PSYCHOTHERAPISTS

Judy Cooper
and
Helen Alfillé

KARNAC

First published in 2011 by
Karnac Books Ltd
118 Finchley Road, London NW3 5HT

British Library Cataloguing in Publication Data

A C.I.P. for this book is available from the British Library

ISBN 978 1 85575 552 9

Edited, designed and produced by The Studio Publishing Services Ltd
www.publishingservicesuk.co.uk
e-mail: studio@publishingservicesuk.co.uk

Printed in Great Britain

www.karnacbooks.com

CONTENTS

ABOUT THE AUTHORS   vii

FOREWORD   ix
Stanley Ruszczynski

PREFACE   xi
Julian Lousada

CHAPTER ONE
Overview of assessment   1

CHAPTER TWO
Are we looking for a diagnosis?   9

CHAPTER THREE
The consultation   17

CHAPTER FOUR
Transference and countertransference in   25
the assessment consultation

CHAPTER FIVE
Contraindications   33

CHAPTER SIX
People who come to us for assessment   41

AFTERWORD   47

REFERENCES   49
INDEX   53

Helen Alfillé is a Senior Member of the British Association of Psychotherapists, a Full Member and Training Analyst of the British Psychoanalytic Association, and a Member of the International Psychoanalytic Association. She is in private practice in London. She is the co-editor of *Assessment in Psychotherapy* (London: Karnac, 1998), and of *Dilemmas in the Consulting Room* (London: Karnac, 2002).

Judy Cooper is a Senior Member of the British Association of Psychotherapists, a Full Member of the British Psychoanalytic Association, and a Member of the International Psychoanalytic Association. She is in private practice in London. She is the author of *Speak of Me as I Am: The Life and Work of Masud Khan* (London: Karnac, 1993), and co-editor of: *Narcissistic Wounds: Clinical Perspectives* (London: Whurr, 1995); *Assessment in Psychotherapy* (London: Karnac, 1998); *Dilemmas in the Consulting Room* (London: Karnac, 2002).

Stanley Ruszczynski

The assessment procedure is a highly charged emotional situation. The patient is in psychological pain and distress and has taken the brave, sometimes desperate, step of seeking help with that emotional state. The patient's sensitivity to his pain and disturbance is likely to be raw, and his presentation of himself is likely to be full of ambivalence. The assessor offers himself as someone who might be able to discern the nature of the patient's distress so as to make a judgement about whether something he knows about, the psychoanalytic process, might offer some assistance. The assessor has the responsibility of meeting the patient's emotional state and sensitively using that experience to carry out the assessment task. To do so, the authors write that "... the assessor needs to provide a safe setting in which a patient can express himself as freely as he is able ...", and, in so doing, often unconsciously recreating aspects of the difficulties which have led to the request for an assessment.

This short book provides a treasure trove of clinical vignettes and conceptual ideas, from a variety of theoretical frameworks and writers, and aims to inform and assist the assessor in the hugely important task of making a judgement about the nature of the patient's distress and the suitability of psychoanalytic treatment.

The assessor has the responsibility of being sensitive to, and reflective about, the complex and multi-layered, conscious and unconscious forces operating in the patient and addressing these sufficiently with the patient so as to assess the suitability of psychoanalytic psychotherapy as the treatment of choice.

Although, of course, in very different ways, both the patient and the assessor are exposed to the powerful emotional forces active in the encounter they are engaged in. The book describes these various dynamic forces from a psychoanalytic perspective, and in doing so introduces, or, for some, reminds, the reader of transference and countertransference phenomena, the examination of which makes up the heart of the assessment process. In taking this perspective with the patient, the assessor gauges the appropriateness of a psychoanalytic treatment and introduces the prospective patient to what such treatment is likely to entail.

The book takes the reader from the initial contact with the patient requesting assessment, through the dynamics of the actual consultation meetings themselves, and addresses the contraindications to psychoanalytic treatment. Although it is stated that the book is written for those assessing for psychoanalytic treatment in private practice, in my view the range of the ideas presented in this book is such that it would also be very helpful to someone making an assessment for possible dynamic work in a public services setting, such as the National Health Service (NHS). What it does very well is promote the idea that *everything* in the assessment encounter needs to be reflected upon and brought into the thinking about the recommendation with regard to treatment. The range of clinical illustrations and theoretical ideas described will alert the reader to much that is likely to emerge in the assessment process.

With the enormous proliferation of different types of psychological treatments, this book is a reminder that dealing with people in distress and developing the capacity to assess for the treatment of choice is a very sensitive, serious, and skilled business. For most patients, the assessment consultation is often the first experience of a psychoanalytic encounter and, as such, needs to be carried out carefully and skilfully. This book provides much that will assist the assessor in doing so.

Julian Lousada

I have always been troubled by the lack of attention paid to assessments in the training of psychoanalytic psychotherapists. It seems
to me that it is an essential tool for the clinician, as well as being
central to the "safety" of the patient. The initial experience is
equally important to both. The patient can only make a genuine
choice to enter therapy on the basis of an experience of what
it might involve emotionally. The therapist has a similar dilemma.
How can a therapist thoughtfully decide to offer a treatment
unless they are confident of their own ability to conduct an assessment?

The book is not a guide in the normal sense of the word. It
makes the reader aware of the complexity involved in assessment.
Both the clinician and the patient have to tolerate what the other
does not know and what they themselves cannot understand. It is
the process of navigating this uncertainty that can reveal some
glimpses of the unconscious configurations in the internal world of
the patient.

The authors use the term "assessment consultation" to encom-
pass the two tasks of having an experience and making a judgement. It is the data from both that can provide some indication as

to whether psychoanalytic psychotherapy is "the treatment of choice".

Central to the book is the assertion that an initial consultation involves two people, each making an assessment of the other, while negotiating their different roles. To lose sight of the importance of the patient's assessment of the clinician, *and his or her method,* undermines one of the essential dynamics of the assessment encounter. This, in turn, poses the question as to what weight should be given to the patient's assessment. It is not altogether obvious how to decide whose judgement should prevail in the face of disagreement.

One of the assessment tasks is to establish a dialogue between the expectations and hopes of the patient and what the clinician imagines is possible.

This book will help readers to think more carefully about the importance and complexities of this aspect of our work. It will be of considerable use to the training process and to those in practice in whatever setting.

I wrote some lines describing you
As though I had brought
                    a kind of clarity
To bear on your experience,
As though something, in verse,
Of what you cannot say
                    was made
Articulate.

(From "Lines", by A. C. Jacobs)

CHAPTER ONE

Overview of assessment

The assessor and his role

Assessment for psychotherapy forms a large part of the clinical work of a consultant psychotherapist, but it raises more uncertainty and anxiety than any other subject in psychoanalytic psychotherapy. [Garelick, 1994]

Given that Garelick talks in terms of the assessor being a consultant, we find it somewhat perturbing that many people expected to do assessments in various settings frequently have very little therapeutic experience. For a therapist, meeting a new patient evokes feelings of suspense, excitement, and anxiety. He is aware of potential dangers in getting in touch with the unconscious in both himself and the patient. He needs to be able to identify with the patient and, at the same time, maintain his analytic role. Within this role, if assessing to refer on to a colleague, he needs to be prudent in what he expects from the patient, aware that an imminent ending is there from the beginning. He needs to put his narcissism aside and leave the centre of the stage. The role of the assessor has broadened over time from being purely a matter of deciding whether a person was suitable for psychoanalytic work to one where the assessor may recommend another form of treatment. Advising a patient in this way could be seen as being in conflict with the aims of psychoanalysis, one of which is to open up choices for a patient and give him control over his own life. Because of this, some therapists consider that asessment is a clinical skill in its own right, with its own technique. It is an introduction to a very different way of relating, both formal yet intimate. In any event, increasingly it is being recognized that clinicians need a considerable amount of experience and expertise in order to develop their individual style and focus in conducting an assessment consultation.

What is an assessment?

In this book, we are talking primarily about assessment for psychoanalytic work in private practice. From our experience, we feel that a minimum of one and a half hours is necessary for an assessment, if the assessment is restricted to one session only.

However, we have come to the conclusion over the years that in order to really understand how a patient uses the setting, at least two consultations are more helpful. Although we are, in general, referring to private practice, it is important to mention that clinicians in other settings may work with other models; for instance, with extended assessment, as was sometimes practised at the Anna Freud Centre, or where an organization pays for a limited number of sessions, it may be more helpful to think of these in terms of an extended assessment rather than ongoing psychotherapy. As Bolognini (2006) says, assessment consultations should be "aimed at clarifying the patient's suffering, needs, ways and levels of functioning, difficulties, fears, motivations, expectations and real possibilities for change" (p. 25). An assessment consultation can be seen as an unequal meeting between two strangers, where one person is troubled and seeking help and the other is informed and trained to listen in a very particular way.

It is not a social chat. One must bear in mind that fantasies have developed the moment a person obtains the name of an assessor, or even before, when someone becomes aware that he wants help.

Some people carry around a piece of paper with the name and number of the assessor for a considerable time, which can be seen as a talisman or transitional object, before making contact. The voice on the telephone both increases fantasies and also gives a modicum of reality to the situation.

Perhaps it is worth remembering that this first unseen, aural contact between patient and assessor on the telephone is a repetition evocative of one of the earliest prenatal links between infant and mother. This experience may be replicated in future therapy with a patient on the couch. As can be seen, the transference and countertransference is intrinsic to the situation and the therapist will be aware of this and use the nuances in the consultation. A patient, having spoken to the assessor on the telephone, on subsequently meeting her said, "Oh, but you sounded so young on the phone." Her transference response of surprise and disappointment was taken up by the assessor. A strong countertransference response to a patient's angry, aggressive, initial phone call alerted the therapist to what might emerge in the consultation. She made sure that there would be someone else in the vicinity should there be any acting out by the patient. An assessment should reflect a microcosm of a patient's life and inner world. It also gives the patient an experience of the analytic setting. It is to be hoped that the containment of the therapeutic setting will allow us to get as full a picture as possible, so that we can begin to assess a patient's capacity to use psychoanalytic work, with its emphasis on the unconscious. The kind of things we need to cover are: what has brought the patient for help *now*, current problems and relationships, and his memories and experiences of early family life and growing up. We will note if there is some evidence of a good primary object. A young woman seeking psychotherapy had been abused by her father from a very early age. The mother denied it until the girl was fourteen, when there was a court case and the father was sent to prison. There were no grandparents and no evidence of a good object, reflected in desperate and empty adult relationships, posing questions in the assessor's mind as to her capacity to enter into a psychoanalytic relationship. We explore loss and the patient's capacity to mourn, any addictions, suicidal attempts or thoughts, somatizing, fantasies, and dreams. We try to cover these themes, but, of course, it is impossible to achieve all this in one session.

What can an assessment offer?

We do not offer a magical cure. We hope that improvement will occur as part of the exploration. Tyson and Sandler (1971) felt that the psychoanalyst was in the difficult situation of seeing a cure as a desirable by-product of the process of analysis but not necessarily the main aim. Freud felt that one of the main aims of analytic work was to enable the patient's unconscious drives to become conscious, so that he might have more choice and control over his actions. "Where id was ego shall be." There are many today who feel psychoanalysis is *passé*, with its painstaking techniques of reflection and exploration. But, in fact, the theoretical concepts are the basis for many of the myriad therapies being offered today that seem to suggest a rapid solution even to complex problems, which seems to us more in keeping with the somewhat unrealistic demands and expectations of today's culture.

A patient's fantasies of what therapy may offer also need to be explored in an assessment. Not everybody is as clear as Fairbairn's patient was when he said that he was not interested in the analyst's interpretations; he was there in search of a father. Many patients are not as clear as to what they are searching for, though "the fact that the patient has chosen to consult a psychoanalyst suggests that probably he is already unconsciously inclined to proceed further along the psychoanalytic route" (Quinodoz, 2003, p. 119). She goes on to note that there may be a latent request for a deeper exploration behind the manifest one. In any event, the patient needs to become aware of the existence of the unconscious and their own internal world. In fact, psychoanalytic psychotherapy offers an opportunity to mature and to integrate. Putting confused feelings into words in an assessment can help to put them into better perspective. The consultation can provide a safe space where patients can be heard. Sometimes, the initial session can prove to be sufficient help in itself, and the patient can move on without a referral: it is as if he needed to tell his story, feel heard and understood, which enabled his perspectives to shift. "Whew, that was such a load off my mind," said one such patient.

The setting

In an assessment, the setting is of paramount importance, as in all psychoanalytic work. After the auditory impact mentioned before, the first visual impression of the psychotherapist in the consulting room is crucial. A young woman who felt physically and emotionally messy and unacceptable saw an analyst whose room was chaotically untidy, reflecting her own experience of chaos. This proved to be unbearable, and she found another analyst where she felt more contained.

Sometimes, patients having therapy in an institution form an attachment to the place, to a "brick mother" rather than the person of the therapist, and even in private practice, a severely deprived patient may form an immediate transference attachment to the setting, as it feels safer. For example, one young man commented, "I like you, but I really love your room." It is of paramount importance that the assessor should be absolutely clear about the parameters of this first setting that the patient encounters. The physical space of the consultation, as well as the appearance and manner of the psychotherapist, will be intensely observed and used by the patient. How they register the place and person of the therapist will be influenced by their fantasies, which, in turn, will affect the material that emerges.

Having had a previous assessment, one woman observed that although she had liked the therapist, she felt more secure and safe with the "solid furniture" of the present assessor's room.

The analytic position

In an assessment, just as in long-term psychotherapy, we have to be aware of our analytic position at all times, which is so different from normal social exchange: "What is distinctive about psychotherapy is the therapist's prohibition upon himself from enacting either the promptings of his own inner world or those of his patient . . ." (Temperley, 1984, p. 102). If we did respond to the promptings of the patient, we may play a part in an enactment, thus distorting our therapeutic role and function of analysing the transference. Much of our training helps us to learn to hold back and not respond to a patient's wishes.

Who comes?

Patients are referred from many different sources. They may make a self-referral, or be referred by GPs, ex-patients, psychiatrists, psychologists, social workers, family, or friends.

Not all these referrers are knowledgeable about what exactly psychoanalytic psychotherapy has to offer. Since Freud, the type of presenting problem has changed dramatically and the basis on which people are referred has broadened considerably. The scope has increased to include not only the "good neurotic", but also narcissistic and borderline patients, often with severe problems in functioning. One also sees many patients with personality disorders who are notably difficult to treat. There is also a group of patients who seek therapy not because of incapacitating symptoms, but because of a wish to explore conflictual issues in a search for personal growth, which may also help their professional development. Distinct from these are those patients who feel they come into therapy only for training purposes, who can be a very defensive and unsatisfactory group to treat. Care is needed in making such a referral, as the resistance is so strong and sometimes implacable.

Timing of the assessment: why now?

As mentioned before, people may hold on to a referral contact for some time. A young woman who kept the telephone number of the assessor in her bag for a year, clearly unconsciously, chose the moment to make contact and arrange her assessment appointment.

Keeping the piece of paper could be seen on different levels: as a talisman to keep her safe, or as a transitional object linking her internal and external worlds. Perhaps it was an indication of her anxiety and ambivalence, all of which would need to be explored in the assessment. A trauma in her current life prompted her to make contact now. The moment was right for her and she was able to make good use of the assessment and her subsequent therapy.

On the other hand, the right moment may be lost. A man who was apparently eager for therapy, came for an assessment just before a long break, during which he instituted changes in his life and decided not to pursue therapy. This could be seen as a defensive flight into health, or a missed opportunity, or it may have provided a sufficient therapeutic experience in itself. In an assessment consultation, it usually emerges quite quickly as to *why now*. Perhaps during or after a difficult relationship a patient may sense a repetition of a pattern. He may feel angry, stuck, or helpless in a given situation, or he may have suffered some trauma, for instance a death, an illness, or loss of a job.

Different conceptual models

In order to reach a formulation as to whether a patient will be able to use psychoanalytic psychotherapy, there are various ways of looking at it. We can think in terms of Coltart's (1993) criteria for suitability, seen primarily in terms of "psychological mindedness". One can assess in terms of ego functioning, looking at coping mechanisms and defences, or, as Winnicott said, there needs to be sufficient ego integration based on good enough early provision. We can look at it, as Zetzel (1968) suggests, in terms of levels of trust, capacity to cope with loss, with the ability to mourn, and to distinguish between inner and outer reality. Or we can see it from the point of view of object relating. Is the person capable of relating in a three-person world, or only in a dyad? In other words, has the patient reached some resolution of Oedipal conflicts, bearing in mind, as Britton said in a lecture, that these conflicts have to be renegotiated in each new relationship. Or, as used to be a more common measure, we can look at libidinal development, looking for the fixation point where a disturbance began: oral, anal, latency, or genital. This may indicate a point of developmental arrest and help to clarify the patient's area of difficulty; for example, addiction would indicate a regression to orality and obsessional behaviour would reflect a degree of anality.

Style of conducting an assessment

There are numerous ways of conducting an assessment, but, for clarity, we will describe two distinct styles. The first is a classical analytic approach, where the assessor does not initiate anything, or tell the patient how to proceed, and does not reassure or respond to any social cues. This preserves strict neutrality and enables the transference, frequently in terms of threatening figures and more paranoid anxieties, to emerge in the session.

This may seem harsh and may be experienced as punitive by the patient, but it does allow access to the areas of disturbance in a very direct way, which can then be explored. This style, without any concessions to forming a therapeutic alliance (for example, not even shaking hands), can be a good indicator for future therapy. Can the patient withstand these strict boundaries and frustrations? On the other hand, an assessor may present him or herself in a more socially conventional way and lead the interview by more actively focusing on symptoms and history, without taking up the opportunity to explore the more paranoid aspect of the material. This second style tends to address the more rational, adult, conscious side of the patient, talking about their difficulties rather than experiencing them in the session. Each assessor develops their own style, often finding their own preferred point along this scale.

CHAPTER TWO

Are we looking for a diagnosis?

Very often, one may embark on an assessment without any clear idea of what one is supposed to come up with by the end of the consultation. Should it be a psychiatric diagnosis, a psychoanalytic categorization, a developmental history? Certainly, together with the patient, we need to reach some mutual understanding of his current predicament, reflecting internal conflicts and early life experience and whether he would benefit from psychoanalytic psychotherapy. Bearing in mind Winnicott's view that psychoanalytic work is for those who need it, who want it, and who can make use of it, the aim of an assessment consultation is to reach a psychoanalytic formulation in order to make an appropriate referral. People frequently come to an assessment deeply troubled, but one must remember that desperation can be a poor indication for psychoanalysis. We are not offering a crisis service. Our objective in a psychotherapeutic consultation is to identify the unconscious phantasies and object relations that characterize the patient's inner life and, consequently, his relationships with other people. It is not simply modelled on a medical or psychiatric diagnosis. A diagnosis is the identification of disease through the patient's symptoms, while a psychotherapeutic assessment is based on a patient telling us his life story and current difficulties and our observation of how he uses the consultation. Diagnosis usually plays a part in arriving at a formulation, but is absolutely essential when faced with acute disturbance, such as florid psychosis, paranoia, suicidal tendencies, perversion, addiction, or the likelihood of violent acting out. This does not necessarily preclude psychoanalytic work, but a referral needs to be carefully considered with an awareness of what the therapist will be dealing with and the possibility of the necessity for medical or psychiatric cover. Diagnosis is primarily based on the objective evaluation of symptoms; we are equally concerned with the healthy part of the patient and whether he has the ego strength to withstand the pain and frustration of psychoanalysis.

One of our main skills is our capacity to observe the relationship between the patient and ourselves which is the beginning of transference. There is no rigid template for an assessment. There are numerous questions to bear in mind, which we are attempting to outline here, but each assessor will develop his own way of conducting and making sense of the consultation. As Tonnesmann (1998) says,

> The patient brings his hopes and his fears to the assessment consultation, the assessor his skills as an experienced psychoanalytic psychotherapist . . . But both patient and assessor also meet as the individuals they are, which means that every assessment consultation evolves as a unique intersubjective encounter. [pp. xi–xii]

It also presents an opportunity for the patient to assess the analyst. It should always be remembered that one must do no harm to a patient, that an assessment should be therapeutic and not traumatic, and, above all, that it should make sense to the patient. Freud (1905a) said "One should look beyond the patient's illness and form an estimate of his whole personality". Quoting Wallerstein (1989), who found, from the 1956 Research Project of the Menninger Foundation:

> Psychoanalysis is the therapy of choice where ego strength, anxiety tolerance, intelligence and capacity for developing insight are of requisite degree and where the neurotic conflict is sufficiently intense and pervasive that satisfactory resolution can only come . . . through the development of the transference neurosis . . . [pp. 563–593]

The human psyche is complicated and multi-layered: for instance, a phobia may be found in an hysterical, or obsessional patient, someone with depression, perversion, addiction, or paranoia. For Freud, the cornerstone of psychological health could be measured by a person's capacity to love and to work; Winnicott might well have added a person's ability to play. The analyst or therapist needs to formulate a deeper, broader, more flexible way of meeting with a patient. Some organizations require people to complete an initial questionnaire, which can act as a guide for the patient as to what areas the interview will cover. Frequently, we use a developmental framework to understand a patient's difficulties. Very importantly, we must recognize the difference between Oedipal and pre-Oedipal disturbance, the former being predominantly a three-person neurotic problem, the latter more to do with two-person relating, reflecting severe difficulties in separation and seen in narcissistic and borderline pathology. Even though separation and loss are universal experiences, how someone deals with their own personal mourning is a very important indicator of their psychic development. Another perspective, in developmental terms, looks at the maturity of defences. These range from the most primitive defences, such as splitting, projective identification, idealization, devaluation, denial, and omnipotence, to more neurotic defences, such as obsessionality, intellectualization, and those more ego-syntonic ones such as humour and sublimation.

As we mentioned in Chapter One, Zetzel (1968) looks at analysability in terms of levels of trust, a capacity to cope with separation and loss, and an ability to deal with inner and outer reality. She uses a diagnostic measure for hysteria, where she categorizes hysterics along developmental lines into four sub-groups, with the "good hysteric" at one end of the developmental spectrum and the "so-called good hysteric" at the other. The former has a hold on reality which is firm, but suffers from an Oedipal inhibition of desire. The latter can be said to be looking for the breast, or, as Bollas (2000) says, is driven by the unconscious wish for the mother's acceptance of the patient's early genitality behind her seemingly adult sexual encounters. She may well not meet the main criteria for analysability. A young woman addict, ostensibly craving a relationship, sexualized every encounter with each man she met and pursued one relationship after another in a compulsive way. As each relationship fractured, she wept hysterically on the couch, angry that she never felt nourished or sustained by them, thereby repeating the early rejection by her mother. Another young woman tried to cajole a male friend into having a committed relationship with her. She was petulant that he had chosen a girlfriend whom she thought was far less attractive than she was. He liked her and found her attractive, but was clear that she was just not suitable, although he was not sure why. It would seem that unconsciously he understood that she saw him as a part object, as a breast, rather than as a whole person. In continuing with the developmental model of assessing, Kernberg (1984) emphasizes the diagnostic approach, especially with border-line and narcisstic disorders. For him, the two main developmental tasks of object relations involve the mastery of aggressive impulses and the attainment of object constancy, which means whole object relations. He would say that severely narcissistic patients (schizoid) are rarely suitable for psychoanalytic psychotherapy.

Borderline patients, alternating between idealizing and deni-grating their objects, would require a very careful referral to an experienced practitioner. A middle-aged patient, paid for by an external agency, continually complained about her therapist to the agency, which did not encourage the splitting involved. Although at other times she would idealize her therapist and the help she was getting, which meant that she managed to remain in treatment for the five years that was covered by the agency, the therapist felt certain she would have left therapy much earlier had she been paying for it herself, when the denigration might have made her terminate treatment. Kernberg has a particular set of criteria for diagnosing emotional maturity with regard to being able to use therapy. He looks for identity confusion, reality testing, and ego strength in terms of impulse control, toleration of anxiety, and con-tainment of frustration. According to these criteria, he would go on to recommend psychoanalysis if there is no identity confusion, but a firm sense of reality and a strong ego. He would suggest a more expressive form of psychotherapy with less emphasis on the trans-ference for those with a fragile ego, and supportive psychotherapy for those altogether more vulnerable.

McDougall (1989) outlines various areas to be aware of when assessing a would-be patient, which may not be immediately obvi-ous in a preliminary consultation. She feels a person should have a basic awareness of psychic suffering and be motivated to come for themselves, not to please others. Moreover, if a patient comes with physical symptoms, denying any link with their psychological state, this may not augur well for psychoanalytic treatment. One also needs to consider whether a patient would be able to tolerate the frustrations and austerity inherent in the psychoanalytic setting, and then to consider the willingness of a patient to receive help and accept being dependent. Fonagy and his associates have devised their Adult Attachment Interview, basing it on infant attachment theory, which explores separation anxiety in small children. They are interested in how the patient responds rather than what he says. This may show the strength of the defence mechanisms and serve to illustrate the capacity for reflective functioning that can be seen in the patient's ability to differentiate between himself and the other. This would mean the patient had the ability to think about conflicts and problems objectively, rather than actually experiencing his disturbance in the room.

Diagnostic labels can be severely restricting when considering making a referral. Indeed, Quinodoz (2003) finds it irrelevant as to whether a patient is considered neurotic, psychotic, or borderline. She is more concerned to explore a patient's wish for integration, his capacity to use his transference object creatively, and whether his destructive tendencies are matched with some desire for reparation. She also emphasizes how important it is for the assessor, in her countertransference, to feel she understands, and is comfortable with, the patient's internal world. Furthermore, Freud's emphasis on free association does not easily lend itself to diagnostic classification. Some clinicians prefer not to read any professional reports prior to their own assessment of a patient. Analysts have changed their focus somewhat from signs (things noticed by others), symptoms (brought by the patient), and diagnosis (the name given to a group of signs and symptoms), towards asking what capacities and qualities a patient needs to be able to use analysis. In Coltart's (1988) view, a watertight categorization is not necessarily helpful, "a diagnosis can close the mind". However, she stresses that every detail can contribute to a fuller picture, even the initial phone call and our response to it; by the end of a consultation the assessor should be able to recognize if the patient is obsessional, hysterical, borderline, psychotic, neurotic, or psychopathic. For her, the main criterion for deciding on suitability is psychological mindedness. She has outlined nine qualities that constitute psychological mindedness, of which she feels that a minimum of three or four should be present for a patient to be considered suitable for psychoanalytic work:

1. An acknowledgement, tacit or explicit, by the patient that he has an unconscious mental life. A psychologist who came for an assessment denied the existence of the unconscious and was contemptuous of the assessor for giving no diagnosis. His anxiety was manifest that the assessor may have had a perspective on him of which he was totally unaware.

2. A capacity to give a self-aware history, not necessarily in chronological order. A patient gave an obsessionally clear and detailed history, but, in being completely disconnected from any affect, it seemed likely that he might well not be suitable for psychoanalytic work.

3. A capacity to give this history without prompting from the assessor and with an awareness of its emotional meaning.

4. The capacity to recall memories with their appropriate affect.

5. Some capacity to step back from his story and to reflect on it. Zetzel calls it "availability".

6. A willingness to take responsibility for himself, not displacing or projecting.

7. Imagination as expressed in imagery, metaphors, dreams, identifications with other people, empathy.

8. Some signs of achievement, hope, and realistic self-esteem (ego strength). "He who fails at everything fails at analysis".

9. The overall impression of the development of the relationship with the assessor (transference).

Coltart (1993, p. 72) reminds us that an assessor should not behave like a caricature of an analyst, remaining virtually silent. It has been said that if you just ask questions you only get answers; the assessor needs to provide a safe setting in which a patient can express himself as freely as he is able. This requires the assessor to use his or her own psychological mindedness to create this space, which allows a creative distance composed of "ever deepening rapport" and total objectivity. We need to gauge ego strength as a fundamental indicator of a patient's capacity to form a therapeutic alliance, which is one predictor of suitability, as therapy is often painful, frustrating, and tedious.

Garelick (1994) also makes the important point that we need to assess the patient's capacity to appreciate the experience of being heard and understood and make constructive use of it, rather than spoil the assessment experience by a dismissive or denigrating attack.

Winnicott draws the distinction between aggression and destructiveness: the former being potentially hopeful, linked to creativity, spontaneity, and the life instincts, while the latter is connected with the death instinct, sadism, and innate envy. Ego strength is also indicated by the patient's ability to contain intense anxiety without having to resort to defensive manoeuvres such as eating disorders, alcoholism, drug addiction, or somatizing.

We look at the patient's expectations and whether these are realistic. It may well be that some patients can be educated into understanding the language and process of psychoanalysis. Even if they have been quite unused to thinking in this way, they can gradually become aware of their inner world and the power of the unconscious. We look at his defences, how he protects his ego in the face of anxiety, to give us an indication of how he might use his therapy. A patient came to the consultation armed with her own solutions to her problems, which were both a denial of her vulnerability and a covert attack on the therapist, usurping her role. In being able to interpret this appropriately as her difficulty in trusting anyone to attend to her needs, the session became more alive. So, one of the most important things we are looking for is the way in which a patient relates to his objects. Does he connect in a way that is clinging, attacking, blaming, merging, paranoid, or grateful? This will help us to be aware of what may predominate in the transference. We are concerned to discover the patient's social network, how he uses it, and how much containment it offers. To make a referral of an extremely isolated patient needs immense care, as the assessor would be aware that the therapist might become his sole object for some time. Baker (1980) quotes some research which finds that diagnosis was of no predictive value. However, in this research there were no cases of psychosis, drug addiction, or psychosomatic disorders, though it did include borderline and narcissistic disorders.

Diagnosis is not necessarily a predictor of analytic success. Quality of object relations is a better indicator. Consequently, isolated people or people who constantly quarrel and rupture relationships (personality disorder) may find it difficult to form or sustain a working alliance. However, Greenson (1967) points out, "A reliable diagnosis is often only possible at the end of treatment" (p. 53). We feel that this is particularly true of narcissistic and borderline patients. In fact, our task can be seen as a double one. Within an assessment, we reach a decision including both the diagnostic picture and a psychoanalytic formulation based chiefly on observing the patient's relationship with the assessor. Together, this allows us to decide if a patient can use psychoanalytic work to help him. There seems to be no definitive view of the function of diagnosis in assessment. Is it ultimately a useful predictor of who can make use of psychoanalytic treament? Perhaps the best tool of assessment would seem to be the assessor's observation of her own countertransference response to the interaction in the session.

CHAPTER THREE

The consultation

W hen considering what happens in a consultation, it is very important to know for whom we are doing this assessment. Are we assessing for an organization, for ourselves, or to make a referral? If an assessment is made by a hospital or clinic, there are certain constraints of time and the consequent intensity of work possible, but, on the other hand, there may be the benefit of input by the whole psychiatric team, which would be particularly helpful for severely disturbed patients. If, however, we are looking for a patient for a trainee psychotherapist, we would take extra care in exploring certain areas of the patient's psyche. We would be particularly concerned about ego strength, ability to commit, addictions, suicidal tendencies, and, of course, psychosis.

When does the assessment start?

Is the initial phone call important? Greenson (1967) feels that the initial phone call should be a good example of any future therapeutic work. This entails the analyst's careful listening and interest in the patient, so that he feels that his concerns are being taken seriously. The transference continues to develop as information is conveyed by the voice and accent of the assessor. Patients can be put off, or made more or less anxious, by the therapist's manner. For example, an American analyst chose to take a call from someone requesting an assessment during a patient's session. He was curt with the new referral and succeeded in making both patients feel rejected. We emphasize that a patient should feel that an analyst is as concerned about his welfare on the telephone as he would be in the consulting room. For instance, Greenson quotes a seventy-eight-year-old man whose psychiatrist had died. He had read about psychoanalysis and Greenson, and had rung for an assessment session. Greenson explained that psychoanalysts worked rather differently and he would like to refer him to a trusted psychiatrist colleague. He left the choice to the patient, however, who accepted Greenson's advice and was very pleased with the referral. Another therapist had the experience of being telephoned on a Sunday for an assessment. The caller was in a very difficult domestic situation but it transpired that she already alerted many professionals to her situation and was receiving a great deal of help. To offer an assessment would have added to the confusion of her splitting and reinforced her fantasy of a magical solution rather than encouraging her to use the help she had already mobilized.

It is of paramount importance that the assessor should be absolutely clear about the parameters of the setting during the first consultation. Although an institute offered just one assessment session, a comparatively new assessor offered another session as she felt she needed to explore the material further. At the end of the second session, the patient asked if she could come yet again. It needs to be clearly understood at the start of the assessment session whether the assessor is assessing for himself or to refer on. As we have said, there are different views about how long an assessment session should last. We use a one and a half hour model, which we usually find to be enough to make a referral. Others find they need considerably longer, while some clinicians only use a regular fifty-minute analytic hour. Still others use the model of a longer assessment period extending over some weeks.

It is important to hear each patient's story with no preconceptions and only later to attach meaning to it. To this end, some practitioners would prefer to read any referral notes only after the assessment. One develops one's own style when doing an assessment, which is helpful in providing a structure. With experience, we build an internal model, a template of an ideal of the perfect consultation, which can never be totally realized. It cannot be rigidly adhered to; one can never cover everything, but it provides a framework from which to proceed.

Klauber (1981, p. 144) makes an interesting point in differentiating between the technique of analysis and that of assessment. He points out that the aim of analysis is to free the patient to make his own decisions, but, inevitably, we advise a patient at the end of an assessment, even though we try to enable him to reach his own decision. Klauber also stresses how essential it is to convey to the patient that psychoanalysis is essentially a sensible therapy. After all, in therapy we try to help the patient make sense of his confusion and distortions. For Klauber, it is imperative to focus most of the assessment consultation on the functioning ego. However, this highlights the difference between this approach and that of some other practitioners who believe that one should in no way ameliorate anxiety, but direct the session predominantly to the area of unconscious disturbance.

The assessor's main responsibility is to begin the establishment of a relationship in some depth and explore the main issues in a patient's life. Because of this, an assessment consultation is enormously important. The patient needs to feel safe enough to begin to trust the therapist and, therefore, the process to which he may be committing himself. He must be treated with courtesy and respect. He must feel secure, heard, and understood. The therapist needs to be interested and accessible, not judgemental. In any event, it is necessary to create space to allow the person to find their own way of expressing themselves. As Holmes (1995) says, "A central purpose of the assessment interview is to act as a stimulus to the patient's unconscious". Klauber calls it, "a traumatic event in the life of a patient" (1971, p. 148). Why? It may be seen as an acknowledgement of vulnerability, talking about one's innermost feelings, thoughts, fears, and fantasies.

"Decisive changes for the patient may ensue from this encounter" (Schubart, 1989, p. 423). One could see the aims of an assessment consultation as contradictory; on the one hand, an attempt to get factual information from the patient, and on the other, trying to create a climate in which unconscious material can emerge. As we have mentioned before, if you ask a question you will only get an answer. Of course, the assessor must feel free to ask questions, more than during an ordinary session, partly to see how the patient responds to the question itself and also to the fact that one has asked it. We do need the patient's story and developmental history, but also we need to be able to make a space within the setting for him to explore more unconscious material. Indeed, Quinodoz (2003) does not believe in any formal history taking. She is more concerned with "how this information spontaneously enters the patient's consciousness" (p. 121) and whether the patient can appreciate that it does have a meaning. We need to build a picture of a patient's internal and external worlds, which will include a social and developmental history. This usually starts with his presenting problems, why he is here and why now. From the patient's point of view, the assessment may be experienced as a formulation of his problems, and this clarification in itself can bring considerable relief. For example, a patient who was an only child brought up in a very close relationship with a single mother was very promiscuous. During the assessment consultation, it became evident to both patient and therapist that the promiscuity was her desperate attempt to separate from her mother. It was hoped that the patient would be able to work through this in subsequent therapy. From the assessor's point of view, it is also a question of considering the suitability of the patient for psychoanalytic work. Looked at from an object relations stance, the assessment covers the patient's present life and difficulties, childhood relationships from early infancy, and how this is reflected in the transference relationship in the assessment.

How do we conduct an assessment consultation? After greeting the patient and indicating where he should sit, we nearly always start the session with a simple question, "I wonder why you find yourself here today?", or "What brings you here today?" This generally leads to a description of the problem and conflicts, which we try to interrupt as little as possible, as we want to see how the patient tells his story: is he aware of the effect of the past on the present? Does he have an awareness of self and others? Does he use the object in the telling of his story? Does he involve or ignore the therapist? We may choose to ask some questions to elucidate certain issues. We might then say something like, "I wonder if you can tell me about your current life, such as work, important relationships [if this has not already been presented as part of the problem], friendships, and interests, and then perhaps you could tell me about your childhood and growing up in your family". Everything is interactive in the telling, but if it has not already emerged, we always check possible addictions, particularly drinking, drug taking, and any eating disorders. We also need to ensure that we become aware of any self-harm, risk-taking behaviour, and suicidal thoughts or attempts.

During the history taking, the assessor is looking for various cues: for instance, any early separations or losses and how these have been experienced and dealt with. We notice how the patient talks about key figures in his life, for instance, parents, grandparents, carers, siblings, which may indicate specific areas of difficulty and defence. Does he talk about them with flat affect or hardly mention an important family member? Is there idealization, denial, intellectualization? "Implicit in history taking is the idea that present problems are rooted in the past" (Garelick, 1994). It is salutary to remember Betty Joseph's words, "I suspect that, if the patient has met up with no object in his infancy on whom he can place some, however little, love and trust, he will not come to us in analysis. He will pursue a psychotic path alone" (Joseph, 1985, p. 452).

Looking at his current life, does he have meaningful relationships? How does he talk about his relationships, and does it seem as if he can experience real intimacy? Has he had any previous therapy, and how does he feel about the experience and the therapist? How is he responding to the assessor, in terms of the more conscious therapeutic alliance and the unconscious transference? What are his expectations of therapy; are they magical in terms of an instant solution, or more reality based? The cross-cultural context also needs consideration in both the assessment and possible referral. The same incident may be differently understood according to a patient's cultural background; for example, a man and woman being alone together in a room, as may happen in psychotherapy, can be construed quite differently in different cultures. In the same way, accepting help from a female therapist, openly talking about sexuality, having to conform to psychotherapeutic boundaries, can all be understood differently and may seem inappropriate within some cultures. In order to be able to reach a decision about a patient's suitability for psychoanalytic psychotherapy, as well as a detailed history taking, we need to explore a patient's inner world. The consultation must include the patient's story and his current circumstances, relationships, and support network, development, including psychosexual development and family life, dream life, major losses, and trauma, main areas of aptitude and interest, and through this composite picture we hope to be able to make an appropriate referral. It is important to be able to distinguish psychiatric disturbance. Psychosis, substance abuse, addictive behaviour, eating problems, or suicide attempts may amount to severe pathology, but may not invariably be total contraindications for psychotherapy. A young woman who had a history of psychiatric breakdown and hospitalization nevertheless did gain much insight with psychoanalytic work. She has become increasingly autonomous and more able to take responsibility for her own destructive tendencies, although she is still liable to view situations in a paranoid way. At the onset of therapy, the therapist ensured that there was adequate psychiatric support for the patient's medication and should she need to be hospitalized. The assessor had clarified what was needed in order to make a realistic referral.

Finally, if we think a patient is suitable for psychoanalytic work, we explore this with him. We give an outline of what therapy involves, including frequency, use of the couch, the fundamental rule of free association, reporting of dreams as a way of understanding the unconscious, responsibility for sessions, fees, and breaks. Regarding fees, the question of who pays for treatment can be crucial; for example, a mother paying for an adult son, a sister paying for her sister, a disturbed patient who makes sure that her father pays the bill. What difference does paying a fee make? Who has control of the treatment? What of patients who pay no fee on the National Health Service (NHS)? Can this encourage a patient to remain infantile, or, if a parent pays, can this interfere with the treatment or even jeopardize it? We ask the patient if he has any questions, and then to think about the session and our recommendation and to get in touch with us if he wants a referral.

If we feel that a patient is unsuitable for psychoanalytic work, we should always offer some other option, possibly getting a psychiatric assessment or seeing their GP. It is essential that a patient comes to psychotherapy of his own volition, not because of pressure from a partner, family, or friends, and not to placate someone: for example, the assessor, the GP, the parents, or partner. From the assessment session, we must decide whether to offer a referral for psychoanalytic psychotherapy, or, if not, what other referral may be appropriate. In order to do this, we search for indications of suitability, bearing in mind contraindications. We look for an awareness of unconscious motivation, the ability to use an interpretation, and to talk about fantasies and dreams. In other words, we are looking for some indication of psychological mindedness. We note how the patient deals with affects such as anger, sadness, anxiety, and frustration. How has he coped with loss? Has he been able to mourn appropriately and move on? How does he cope with a silence in the consultation?

We try to assess ego strength, as psychoanalytic psychotherapy can be difficult, frustrating, and painful. We look at the defences that the patient uses and his ability to tolerate feelings of guilt. In essence, has he reached the Kleinian depressive position with the ability to tolerate feelings of ambivalence towards the object? Of course, in assessing ego strength, we also need to note the areas where the patient functions well, is conflict free, and has a sense of confidence and achievement. This is particularly important, because, if someone has been unable to complete or achieve anything, it is unlikely he will have the basis on which to build a successful therapy. This includes work, relationships (how does he treat and use his objects?), reality testing (is the boss out to get him?), and the severity of symptoms (what do they cost him? how rigid and incapacitating are they?). Perhaps we are so used to experiencing our patients' harsh and critical superegos that we find it difficult to hold on to more positive experiences, such as the enjoyment of a close relationship, or satisfaction in work and its rewards. Can he alternate freely between inner and outer reality and recognize the difference? Can he move back and forth in historical time and make connections while relating his history? Above all, is he curious to explore the reasons why he finds himself coming for psychotherapy now? In the assessment session, we try to pick up all the cues the patient gives us, verbal, non-verbal, and visual, in order to help us predict whether we think he has the capacity to use the therapeutic process creatively. This can include apparently unimportant exchanges such as whether a patient expects to shake hands or how he addresses you. We observe how he presents himself to a stranger in an unusual situation, his body language, and whether he asks to use the lavatory, requests a glass of water, or even, more unusually, asks to use the telephone.

If questionnaires are used as a preliminary requirement, what does this add? It may allow the assessor to avoid some direct questions, but the disadvantage to this could be that it deprives the assessor of hearing the full story in the patient's own words. Having prior access to information about a patient alters the framework. Expectations on both sides are affected by this. The patient may feel it unnecessary to tell parts of his story which he has already written about, and the therapist may wait for an important part of his history which is not forthcoming. In either event, the spontaneity may be compromised. On the other hand, questionnaires can be useful in a structure such as the British Association of Psychotherapists Reduced Fee Scheme, where there are very specific requirements for eligibility to meet the needs of trainees. As in all areas of therapeutic work, it is important to give patients options and the reason for the questionnaire should be stated clearly.

We offer the patient the space and time to tell his story. We need to listen carefully to the way in which the story unfolds. The way he relates to the assessor, and the assessor's response to this, whether positive, negative, or with detachment, give an indication of any future therapeutic work. It includes both transference, countertransference, and therapeutic alliance. Whatever emerges from the consultation, the most important thing is for the patient to have an authentic experience.

CHAPTER FOUR

Transference and countertransference in the assessment consultation

... transference refers to the relationship that develops between
patient and analyst as a result of projection onto the analyst of feelings, thoughts, and attitudes that derive from the childhood past of
the patient and from his relationships to important objects that
have undergone repression. [Shapiro, 1984, p. 13]

W aelder (1960) emphasizes that the chief feature of transference is the effort by the patient to persuade the analyst to behave as if he were an object from his past.
Transference can be seen as a ubiquitous phenomenon, as all our
relationships are coloured by our earliest experiences of object relations. "One might say that this is the transference of everyday life"
(Shapiro, 1984). It follows that transference reactions occur in all
patients undergoing psychotherapy and, therefore, it is of the
utmost importance to be sensitive to the transference–countertransference manifestations within the assessment exchange. Having
said this, it is important to stress that Freud used this concept as a
particular phenomenon occurring in analysis and reaching its
fullest expression in the transference neurosis. The transference
which develops in treatment manifests as a "stuck" transference,

which is different from the transference reactions of everyday life. According to Freud, impulses that have never before been conscious may surface for the first time. If patients are caught in this kind of transference in therapy, for example, "in love" or "in hate", it is a resistance which Freud initially saw as an obstacle to the treatment. Later, in his paper "The dynamics of transference" (1912b), he describes the process as "This struggle between the doctor and the patient between intellect and instinctual life, between understanding and seeking to act, is played out almost exclusively in the phenomena of transference". It became a central dynamic in the treatment process. This is why it is so important for the assessor to be sensitive to these nuances, because it gives a taste of how the transference relationship may develop during the course of therapy. Some practitioners differentiate between the first piece of evidence of transference seen in an assessment consultation, which they term "false transference" (Bird, 1972; Zetzel, 1970) or "pre-treatment pseudo-transference fantasies" (Zetzel, 1970) and the gradual development of the transference in treatment. The sort of things we are looking for as transference phenomena would obviously occur more clearly in the ongoing therapeutic relationship, but some may be evident in the assessment session.

Greenson (1967) considers there are various characteristics that typify transference phenomena. He lists inappropriate responses based on the repetition of the past, intensity, ambivalence, capriciousness, and tenacity/lack of spontaneity. It is interesting to note that originally Freud thought that transference does not occur in psychotic patients, but Rosenfeld (1969) has emphasized that transference is experienced by these patients; the problem is "recognizing and interpreting schizophrenic transference phenomena" (Sandler, Dare, & Holder, 1973, p. 54), "As soon as the schizophrenic approaches any object in love or hate, he seems to become confused with this object . . ." (ibid.). This is like a baby unable to distinguish between me and not-me. Even the most disturbed patient has windows of rationality. In a transference psychosis, problems are experienced more concretely and are concentrated on the analytic treatment situation.

Turning to the countertransference, we can define it in various ways: (1) the analyst's unconscious (repressed, distorted, inappropriate, and unanalysed) attitude to the patient, treating the patient as an early transferential object. In this context, Winnicott (1960) describes it as the analyst's "neurotic features which spoil the professional attitude and disturb the analytic process as determined by the patient" (Sandler, Dare, & Holder, 1973, p. 64); (2) the analyst's response to the patient's transference (i.e., a response to what the patient evokes in him); (3) the whole of the analyst's attitude and behaviour towards the patient. Throughout the history of psychoanalysis, transference and countertransference (they are inseparable; counterparts) have been regarded as potentially dangerous. These concepts emphasize the need for a rigorous personal analysis for practitioners that makes psychoanalytic-based therapies unique.

Freud's original idea of countertransference corresponds to the first definition, but some clinicians eagerly followed Heimann's second definition (1950), which stressed the patient's pathology and put the onus on the patient, rather than the analyst having to own any part in the exchange. Greenson (1974, p. 259) says, "Every psychoanalyst experiences many shades and degrees of love, hate, and indifference towards each of his patients". This range of feeling is intrinsic to the analytic process, and the difficulty of using them appropriately in the treatment confirms the need for a thorough personal analysis and training so that the therapist is more able to respond objectively to what the patient brings, rather than to vestiges of the therapist's own unresolved issues.

Greenson (1965) developed a distinction between transference and the working alliance, which he describes as "the relatively non-neurotic relationship to the analyst", as opposed to "the more neurotic transference reactions". However, some strict Kleinians do not recognize these distinctions and interpret all material in terms of the here and now transference and the projections and introjections allied to this. They tend not to communicate with the integrated ego and do not use the concept of the working alliance.

As mentioned before, Freud came to see transference as an essential part of the therapeutic process, "Finally every conflict has to be fought out in the sphere of transference" (1912b, p. 104). Of course, transference takes place in everyday life, but the objectivity of the analyst, "his refusal to play along with the patient's preconceptions or to respond in accordance with his expectations creates a novel situation" (*ibid.*) whereby the analyst can interpret to the patient that he is behaving as if the analyst were his parent or other significant person from his past. The importance of a rigorous training cannot be emphasized too strongly when we recognize the inevitability of a patient drawing one in to enact their original conflicts with their primary objects and the need to be vigilant about this. A supervision session enabled a therapist to realize how she was treating a very disturbed patient in both an over-protective and yet also rejecting way, like the patient's own mother. By extension now, countertransference is seen as the emotional response of the analyst to his patient. As such, it is a potentially sensitive indicator of the transference, as the analyst must use his emotional response as a key to the patient's unconscious. The analyst must be able to contain feelings stirred up in him, as opposed to discharging them as does the patient.

The tremendous importance of the initial transference to the assessor must be taken into account in any future therapy. The assessment consultation is likely to be an enormously important experience for the patient. There are those who believe that a real transference only develops within an established treatment relationship. Many others think that the transference relationship has already begun to emerge from the moment help is sought. This has been variously described, as we previously mentioned, as a "false transference", "pre-treatment pseudo-transference fantasies" (free-floating transference), so one has to decide whether one wants to make a transference interpretation in the assessment consultation or not. A transference interpretation may serve to confront the patient with more unconscious aspects of himself and, in so doing, help him to modify his idealization of the assessor at the end of the consultation. Of course, it could also enhance the positive transference to the assessor. This needs to be sensitively judged. Nevertheless, the transference should be positive enough to be considered a point of reference for the patient should his future therapy run into any difficulty or should he need to return for further consultation for any reason. For example, a patient was assessed and referred to a therapist who subsequently retired early, leaving the patient frustrated and furious. His therapist suggested he contacted the assessor, but forgot to tell the assessor this. Although he was willing to do this, as the assessment had been a positive experience, the assessor did not remember him, and her countertransference compounded his sense of rejection, which had its origins in his early infancy. Another example of a positive assessment transference is a man who returned to his assessor after three years in a group, was then referred to a therapist, but subsequently found himself on the tube going to the assessor's station, ostensibly on his way to his new therapist.

An assessor needs to be fully aware of the patient's transference, which can be very powerful and durable. We know of one patient for whom the assessor represented the critical, problematic mother. She went on to a difficult but ultimately successful therapy where she found her good object, still holding on to the negative transference to the assessor as the bad mother. Eventually, she was able to integrate this splitting. In a consultation, the analyst should, ideally, represent at least some aspects of a new object for the patient so that he does not feel isolated in what may seem to be an all too familiar anxiety-provoking situation. It is, therefore, of paramount importance to observe very closely the responses of the patient to anything we say. Of course, in a consultation, the patient always uses the chair and can, therefore, monitor the analyst's expressions very carefully, which can give us further insight into the transference picture. Thus, there is a difference between assessing to refer a patient and assessing to take on the patient oneself. In the latter there is no one to carry out the "gate keeping" function (Schachter, 1997) and a full-blown transference relationship can begin to emerge from the start.

The feelings evoked in the assessment will always appear somewhere in the subsequent treatment. As mentioned before, the transference and countertransference start well before the initial meeting. Greenson (1992) emphasizes the importance of the initial telephone call as being the start of the transferential relationship for both patient and analyst. Hinshelwood (1995) makes the point that the assessor should make it clear from the beginning if he is not to be the therapist, if therapy is indicated. Schachter (1997) emphasizes that there is a difference between an assessment consultation and ongoing therapy, although, of course, there are also commonalities. She feels that one must be careful about making transference interpretations in an assessment when the assessor is not going to be the therapist. She also feels that much of the patient's life history will remain unexplored if too much emphasis is put on the transference relationship. However, in the face of transference resistance, that is, a negative or paranoid transference which is immediately very intense, it must be interpreted to avoid a stalemate. A therapist assessed a very angry man with poor impulse control who became verbally abusive when she suggested that he was unsuitable for a private referral. Although she did interpret his negative feelings, he left enraged, not accepting the offer of a more containing referral and threatening to report her. With some patients, it becomes apparent that transference manifestations are part of their story and these, together with our countertransference responses, facilitate the telling of their story. Mrs P arrived at her assessment consultation very early, which the therapist commented on. This led Mrs P to feel rejected and unwelcome, prompting her to recall her anguish at her mother's early death.

A transference interpretation can definitely be useful in an assessment consultation if one views it in part as a kind of mini session, giving a taste of work to come and helping with the assessment for suitability for treatment. None the less, one must remember that the minute the patient enters the consulting room he is graphically conveying the essence of himself through his appearance, his clothes, his bearing, and presentation, to which we will surely have a countertransference response. Schachter (1997) gives a very good example of a patient given to somatizing and going the rounds of medical care, who eventually arrived for an assessment consultation "carrying the signs of her ill, fragile state in the form of two large cushions, one of which she placed behind her back, the other on her lap supporting her arms" (p. 60). She was dressed in black with a surgical neck collar. Any attempt to discuss relationships produced an angry and contemptuous response, provoking a strong negative countertransference in the therapist, who felt she just wanted to get rid of the patient but who began to understand the vulnerability and anxiety underlying the hostile transference of the patient, which, on further exploration, seemed to be a re-experiencing of a neglectful, abandoning mother.

Of course, these countertransference feelings are in direct response to the patient's transference, and can help to provide invaluable information as to the suitability of the patient for psychoanalytic therapy. Certain transference reactions may indicate that someone could be resistant to the therapeutic process. We need to be particularly mindful of an idealized transference reaction, since it could indicate a transference neurosis which never allows the exploration of the underlying hostility. Or consider an obsessional or schizoid patient, both of whom respond to the world through intellectualization and might express this in an assessment in an attempt to control or blank out the therapist. If we are able to pick this up in the consultation, it would be very helpful in deciding about a referral. For instance, we may feel, that the patient will need a period to thaw out from his frozen state, as indicated by Fenichel (1946) before being able to use psychoanalytic work. In the same way, we may be able to pick up chronic acting out from the transference behaviour (impulse ridden, addictive, erotized) of the patient or our countertransference responses (irritated, overwhelmed, feeling controlled).

Just as an assessment patient can feel they would like to continue with the assessor as their therapist, so we sometimes feel an immediate rapport with a patient. It is a fact that one responds more instinctively to some people, and this shows how essential it is to be aware of countertransference issues, particularly when being drawn to a patient can be evidence of a possible manipulation and seduction. Thus, an immediate identification with the patient may well have implications and complicate the subsequent choice of therapist and therapy. A supervisee presented a patient who arrived for a consultation saying that he was far too clever and complicated to come into therapy; his lofty omnipotence produced strongly negative countertransference feelings in the therapist, which, on further investigation, were recognized as her own early experience with an older brother (countertransference in its original sense of an unconscious block or unconscious difficulty in oneself that is the therapist's transference) that prevented her from understanding the patient's use of grandiosity to defend against painful feelings of loss and abandonment.

CHAPTER FIVE

Contraindications

Psychoanalysis has developed from the early days when Freud (1904a, 1905a, 1912e, 1937c) felt that narcissism, psychosis, and certain character weaknesses and defects were contraindications for analysis, as he believed these patients would be unable to form a transference relationship. Now, we recognize how difficult it is to make such a clear-cut distinction, as some patients have aspects of both neurosis and psychosis: Hopper's (1991) "encapsulated pathology". Moreover, Freud excluded deeply rooted depression and states of confusion, as well as patients aged over fifty. He believed this last group of patients would be too rigid and their capacity for intrapsychic change would be severely curtailed. Again, today, we think very differently; for instance, we not only have people over fifty, but over seventy. This is hardly surprising, as it is part of the socio-political climate of the day. For Freud, assessment for psychoanalytic suitability was based on the classical medical model; hence the use of the term indication and contraindication. The former is used to suggest the most appropriate treatment of the illness based on symptoms and the patient's history. Contraindication refers to the unsuitability of the form of treatment. Our assessments are based on the distinction between what the patient complains of (symptoms) and our observations (the signs that we pick up). It may be useful to note that symptoms are not so confined to a diagnostic category as we used to believe: for example, depression, phobias, and obsessions can be a feature of many assessment profiles. However, during an assessment session, we need to be very aware of possible contraindications for psychoanalytic work. We believe the only category which would completely rule out the possibility of this type of therapy is organic brain disease, although now even this is open for discussion; for instance, the neuropsychoanalyst Mark Solms has suggested that a modified version of psychoanalytic psychotherapy could be useful with some patients in this category. Ogden (1989) believes that we would do a patient a disservice if we embark on treatment aware that we do not like him. Although one might feel that it should be possible to analyse an initial negative countertransference response, in practice Ogden feels that it imposes an added burden on the beginning of treatment if there is an intense negative transference or countertransference.

He also cautions against starting treatment if there is an immediate erotic transference or countertransference. So, our title of contraindications needs to be expanded upon to include a broader spectrum of suitability/unsuitability and indications and contraindications. There is an overlap which can lead to some confusion between indications/contraindications and criteria of suitability/unsuitability. A young man whose anxiety led to a pattern of sabotaging many aspects of his life repeatedly found himself in dependent and extremely angry and resentful relationships. This resulted in frequent job loss. He might have been considered suitable for psychoanalytic treatment, but, due to his lack of any comprehension or insight into his internal conflicts (Coltart's "psychological mindedness", 1988), he would have been inaccessible to any measure of self-awareness and, consequently, this sort of treatment would be contraindicated at present. Or, as Tyson and Sandler (1971, p. 215) said, an obsessional neurotic might "constitute an indication for psychoanalysis, but the presence or absence of certain qualities in the patient might render him unsuitable for the treatment or the treatment unsuitable for him".

Another example is of a professional woman who, on the face of it, appeared suitable and who could make insightful connections, but whose early deprivation was so great that psychoanalytic treatment seemed to intensify her lack of any good object; a reassessment found that a therapeutic community could provide a more holding environment. In fact, she did not take this up. Gross neglect or serious deprivation in the first two years of life is frequently a contraindication, as there is no good object to provide a base on which to build.

Even if a patient seems suitable in that he has conflicts which are causing him pain and getting in the way of his leading his life satisfactorily, he still may not be accessible to psychoanalytic work if he is unable to form the necessary treatment alliance, which involves the capacity to tolerate frustration, a minimal degree of objectivity and separateness, and a modicum of basic trust and belief in the aims of treatment. Limentani (1989) warns assessors that patients whom they feel will be able to make a firm treatment alliance may turn out to have a hard core of basic mistrust that constantly sabotages the therapy and everything else. Most therapists would not agree with Langs, who stated in 1982 that a therapist had an ethical duty to take into therapy all patients who came to him. An assessor should treat certain symptoms with extreme caution. This would include a person with florid symptoms of psychosis, evidence of possible physical violence or self-destructive behaviour, extreme forms of addiction, and entrenched somatization. Although severe somatic manifestations such as the "Chicago seven" (bronchial asthma, gastric ulcer, hypertension, rheumatoid arthritis, ulcerative colitis, neurodermatitis, and thyrotoxicosis) used to be considered to have no symbolic meaning so psychoanalysis was not indicated, today many can accept that these nonverbal "signifiers" can be used to understand early pathology and lead the way to more verbalized symbolic communication, such as dreams and fantasies, in the therapeutic treatment.

Serious perversion may need a specialist clinic, such as the Portman. These symptoms would not necessarily preclude us from referring such a patient, but, in these instances, more than ever, we cannot have any omnipotent therapeutic illusions. Flexibility is needed, and the assessor may decide to refer the patient to a therapist who works alongside a team (hospital, clinic, GP practice), and to be aware of the dangers of splitting and the need to contain this.

Lucas, a psychoanalyst experienced with psychotic patients, in a lecture, emphasizes the importance of communication with a spouse, parents, or nurses of a psychotic patient, as they are the ones dealing with him. Zetzel is clear that the so-called good hysteric is not a good prospect for psychoanalytic work. She believes that two or more of the following criteria, together with a tendency towards a regressive transference, should set up warning signals:

1. absence or significant separation from one or both parents during the first four years of life;
2. serious pathology in one or both parents, often associated with an unhappy or broken marriage;
3. serious and/or prolonged physical illness in childhood;
4. absence of meaningful sustained object relations with either sex.

Desperation may be more suitable for a crisis service than long-term psychotherapeutic work. An expectation of quick results is not a good indicator for psychoanalytic treatment. In an assessment consultation, one may feel tempted to offer a patient treatment on the basis of compassion, but this is not sufficient for assessing his suitability for treatment. Klauber (1971, p. 155) believes that Freud's criterion of "a fairly reliable character" can be seen as a solid yardstick for a hopeful result of treatment. He also makes the point that psychoanalytic diagnosis is not just a medical, psychiatric diagnosis, but, rather, one that depends on a complex assessment of motives and defences which involve a much deeper and fuller exploration of the personality throughout the patient's whole history. Also, importantly, it must take into account repetition compulsion as an indicator of how the analysis may proceed. He is cautious about patients who try to charm, unrealistic practical arrangements including fees (too low, too high, other people paying), patients who present with only one symptom (for instance, an eating disorder or psychosomatic complaints without other conflicts or anxieties), which could indicate a lack of capacity for varied forms of displacement and perhaps a difficulty with symbolization, and hypochondriacal patients where there is little flexibility and potential difficulty in forming stable relationships. Klauber (*ibid.*, p. 151) emphasizes the importance of the patient's motivation to get better. Consciously, he may seem ready to make a commitment to treatment and to cope with its frustrations. Unconsciously, there may be resistance: repressed wishes, or perhaps the secondary gain of maintaining the status quo, however uncomfortable it seems on a conscious level. Motivation must also be seen in terms of whether a life situation has the possibility of fundamental change (*ibid.*, p. 154).

Limentani quotes cases which have shown poor response to treatment as revealing one common denominator, "a symptom or a life situation which has proved unanalysable" (1972, p. 52). So, we consider motivation an essential indicator of analysability. "Psychoanalytic treatment has nothing to offer the patient who wishes only to be relieved of his suffering" (Kuiper, 1968, p. 263). There must be a genuine desire to get better through self-understanding rather than an unrealistic neurotic motivation to achieve an ideal state; for instance, the woman who expects to be potent like a man as a result of the analysis. Also, that the patient goes into treatment because *he* wants to, rather than being urged to do so by someone else (e.g., parent, spouse, doctor). Baker (1980) says that primitive defence mechanisms, such as splitting, projective identification, denial, idealization, omnipotence, and devaluation are the root causes of ego weakness and, therefore, underlie everything referred to in the literature as constituting contraindications for psychoanalysis.

Holmes (1995) differentiates between absolute contraindication, for instance organic brain disease, and relative contraindication. He feels that a history of at least one good relationship for basic trust and an acknowledgement of positive achievement indicating a capacity for reality testing are good indications for psychoanalytic work. A history of psychotic breakdown, addiction, or destructive behaviour patterns, suggesting poor frustration tolerance, and entrenched somatization are relative contraindications.

In an assessment, the content and style need to be screened for noting how the patient deals with himself and his objects: how does he cope with psychic pain; can he reflect on his inner world? As Kuiper (1968) said, "He who fails in everything probably will also fail in his analysis. . . . A healthy part of the personality is absolutely necessary" (p. 263). Kächele and Thomä (1987), talking of the appropriateness of psychoanalysis, says, "sick enough to need it and healthy enough to stand it".

What do we do with someone who comes for a consultation wanting psychoanalytic therapy but who is manifestly unsuitable for it? We try to suggest an alternative form of treatment, for example, Arbours therapeutic community, or a non-interpretative therapy, a group, psychiatric support, or doctor. A borderline patient found herself feeling confused and increasingly disturbed by the free associative method and was able to work better within the structure of a cognitive–behavioural approach. Perhaps, had her first therapist been able to act as an auxiliary ego within the analytic framework, she may have been able to use a modified form of psychoanalytic work. Although we have so many pointers in our assessment procedure, in many ways the criteria are not clear-cut and to foresee the way any given treatment will progress is extremely difficult. Klauber (1981) warns that although not necessarily contraindicated, for seriously disturbed patients

> . . . the greatest pitfall of analysis is an excesssive belief in our power to reconstitute the character and the best results are still generally to be obtained with those who, in Freud's description, have a fairly reliable character to start with. [pp. 155–156]

Some patients who seem to be unsuitable may have varying degrees of a healthy ego and these assets, rather than their pathology, may be the decisive factor (Greenson, 1967, p. 53). Trivial complaints, as well as wishes of family, friends, and lovers, is a contraindication. So-called scientific curiosity or professional advancement do not augur well, because they are so defensive; likewise, the demand for quick results or gratification through secondary gain. Contradictory and flexible ego functions are required: will the patient be able to regress within a session and recover at the end? Can he renounce some reality testing yet still understand what we are communicating? The patient needs honesty of purpose and integrity; the opposite can sometimes be seen in an assessment. Occasionally, patients have been known to present themselves with a false identity which may indicate a paranoid state of mind that would need to be addressed. The external life situation of the patient needs taking into account. A neurosis may be better than a devastating physical illness. The therapeutic work with a patient with AIDS, of necessity, focused on his need to face the reality of his impending death.

Perhaps we need to conclude by saying that there are no absolutes when looking for contraindications. There are guidelines, but as psychoanalysis develops, these broaden to include wider categories (even some organic brain disease, which Holmes considers a total contraindication, is being researched for modified psychoanalytic work by neuropsychoanalysts such as Mark Solms). We are aware, for instance, that although psychosis was long held to be a contraindication, ". . . analysis can act as a true life line, the only means of survival for some psychotic patients" (Limentani, 1972, p. 71).

CHAPTER SIX

People who come to us for assessment

W e would like to give a few vignettes of people who have come to us for assessment over the years, giving some idea of the range of hopes and fears, anxieties and expectations, and all the fantasies that accompany the courage it takes to make the first move to arrange an assessment consultation.

A therapist was referred a patient by a supervisee. After many months the patient had not telephoned, but the referrer was convinced that at some point he would. Some considerable time after that, the patient made contact. Although his conflicts had been ongoing, something in his life situation triggered his immediate need to telephone. He had kept the therapist's name and number in his wallet all that time. This could be seen as a bridge between inner and outer experience, like Winnicott's transitional object. It is always difficult if someone comes for a consultation at the behest of a parent, partner, child, GP, or any influential other. This might lead to refusal, a passive but resentful acquiescence, or there could be a total denial of need. Very rarely will a patient be able to use psychoanalytic work in such circumstances.

Mrs L has been in psychotherapy for several years, which she has found to be extremely helpful. She was critical of her husband's untrained counsellor and, through her own therapist, found a qualified female therapist for him. He attended a consultation, but decided that he did not wish to leave his counsellor. His ambivalence towards his wife's attempted control was clear from his rejection of the therapist. On the other hand, Mr A recognized how useful his wife was finding her intensive therapy and decided that he would like to explore his own conflicts. He was able to ask his wife to find him a therapist. In his assessment, he articulated problems both in his own personal narrative and his marriage and telephoned a week later to say that he would like to go ahead with starting therapy.

Frequently, we are approached by students in counselling and some therapy courses which require some personal experience of psychotherapy, usually stating a minimum number of sessions required. When asked at an initial consultation why they wish to have therapy, they reply, "Because I have to." They leave the minute they have fulfilled the requirements, usually not able to engage in the process of therapy, terrified of being the patient, preferring to identify with the grandiose fantasy of being the therapist.

A patient telephoned sounding convinced that he wanted psychotherapeutic help. Even from the telephone conversation, the therapist was aware of feeling deeply uneasy. She sensed an underlying aggression in his demand for an assessment. Working in private practice, not within a hospital or clinic team, it was important that she would not feel threatened, so she ensured that she would not be alone in the house during the consultation. It quickly became clear that this patient was indeed quite disturbed. He did not really want an assessment, but omnipotently demanded a referral and seemed unable to hear that the assessor did not consider psychoanalytic work appropriate for him. He demanded to know why, and the therapist told him that in view of his acknowledgment of his difficulties in controlling his anger, she felt that he would not be able to tolerate the frustrations of the analytic boundaries. She wanted to refer him to a psychotherapeutic community, but at this suggestion he lost control, shouting abuse and pacing around the consulting room in an agitated fashion, finally walking out slamming the door. He subsequently wrote a letter of complaint to the Association.

Two completely individual young women with uncertainities about their relationships: one had a much younger boyfriend and the other had a partner with far more limited financial resources than she did. Each came for a consultation thinking they wanted change. However, in both cases, the initial exploration, giving an indication of future analytic work, caused sufficient anxiety about possible loss to enable each one to reassess their feelings and decide to commit to the relationship. The consultation proved to be mutative, and long-term therapeutic work was not indicated at present.

Of course, many people come with difficulties in their personal relationships, either because they do not have a relationship, or due to problems in sustaining intimacy. One example is of women who have pursued a career and an independent lifestyle and have reached a time in their lives when they become aware of their biological clock and their ambivalent wish to have a baby. Often, they feel that therapy will provide the partner and the baby. An attractive woman in her early forties came for an assessment, saying to the assessor that she was in a loving, stable relationship, but "if only therapy could make me find my boyfriend sexually attractive". The assessor, naturally, explored with her the magical expectation and the power and idealization of the therapeutic process. If these women are referred for therapy, part of the ongoing work would be to understand the conflicts which have prevented them from an intimate and procreative relationship.

A man in his forties came for an assessment with a desperate wish for a loving, intimate relationship. The assessor realized, on hearing his story, that this man had never been able to separate from a domineering and demanding mother, which would need to be resolved in therapy before he was able to find an appropriate relationship.

Sometimes, we assess a patient who has had a history of various therapies. There may be a difference between those who have been in psychoanalytic work and someone presenting who has experienced a whole range of different therapies. This may indicate a level of promiscuity reflected in several areas of the patient's life, showing the deep fear of intimacy of the more disturbed patient.

A different scenario is that of a person who comes to us having been in psychoanalytic work before. This could have been a good experience that the patient may draw on with a new therapist at a different stage of his life or a negative experience and/or an unresolved transference. Some people come with a specific problem, some with general malaise, some aware that they are repeating negative patterns of behaviour, and some who feel paralysed. Others may state specific requirements about what they want. This can range from particular qualities in the therapist to whom they are referred in terms of age and gender, such as "I must have someone who knows what it feels like to be over fifty", or "I would like someone who is a mother" to someone who feels the need to control and demands a very particular place and time: "I can only manage 8 a.m. three doors from home!" There can be more intricate demands which need careful thought and may result in different formulations from different therapists. Previously, older patients were considered unsuitable for psychoanalytic-based work. Freud believed that after fifty no real change could take place as the psychic apparatus would be too fixed. Today, age is not the barrier it once was, and we have people in their seventies and even eighties coming for psychotherapy.

A woman in her late seventies was referred following a heart operation. She was deeply depressed. She had suffered many traumatic losses in her life and had lost her will to live, but retained a vestige of hope which she invested in the therapy. For a year she worked once weekly and told her story, but after a dream of a train journey crossing Europe, which had resonance from childhood, she realized that her therapy was an ongoing journey. She increased her sessions to three times weekly, worked through her deep depression, rediscovered her energy for life, and, although she had initially said that she wanted her therapist to accompany her to her death, she was able to leave after six years of therapy, having internalized the good analytic experience. Another older woman, in her early eighties, came following the death of her husband after a long, childless marriage. She was shocked at her own intense sexual feelings which were expressed towards another woman she had known from her childhood. She stayed in a long-term therapy, discovering more about her internal world. Older people also come for therapy with anxieties about ageing and death. A man in his mid-sixties came beset with fear about his failing health and potency and the possibility of dying alone. He is beginning to understand his sense of isolation in terms of his difficulties with intimacy and legitimate identity as a man.

AFTERWORD

Perhaps having an "Afterword" is an unusual format. But we think that although each chapter speaks for itself, there are many questions that arise from the public and from professionals in the area of assessment. Assessment is of such prime importance in helping someone to find the therapy that is best for them.

The recent proliferation of various forms of therapy frequently leads to confusion, not only in the potential patient, but also in the referrer. People often come to us not understanding who we are and what we are offering, and this may not have been clarified by the person referring them. Consequently, we may be thought of as psychiatrist, psychologist, doctor, counsellor, therapist, psychotherapist, or psychoanalyst, without any real understanding of what the different labels mean.

Society has become increasingly complex, with the breakdown of relationships and communities leading to many people experiencing high levels of stress, depression, anxiety, and psychosomatic symptoms. More people are coming for help with expectations of a quick solution encouraged by the promises from several of the therapies being offered today.

It is necessary for us, as psychoanalytic practitioners, to be able to understand what prompts someone to come to us for an assessment. We need to be able to decipher whether the person can use an awareness of unconscious processes and the internal world, and whether he has a capacity to think about himself in a different way. By the end of an assessment consultation, we hope we can clarify with the person whether this may be the beginning of a journey, whether it has had a mutative effect, or whether we need to suggest another form of treatment or help. Was the patient able to use the professional setting of trust, where the past and future is caught up in the here and now of the transference, with the consequent possibility of lifting repression, even if this is not interpreted?

Several questions have occurred to us while writing this guide. What part does intuition play in an assessment consultation? Hinshelwood (1995) talks of an "intuitive hypothesis". How can the assessor come to a conclusion which he can share with the patient? Are we trying to decide what might be the best treatment of choice for the patient, or just explore whether a patient can tolerate and use a psychoanalytic process of enquiry? Are we thinking that the patient is suitable for psychoanalytic-based treatment or that the treatment is suitable for the patient? Increasingly, we have asked ourselves whether one session of assessment is enough. We feel that, ideally, we should offer two sessions in order to gain some idea of how someone uses the initial session.

The assessor needs to be confident in his technique whatever method he has chosen for conducting an assessment consultation. Of course, he gains confidence through experience, but we feel very strongly that all training organizations should include assessment in their training curriculum. Very often this has been neglected, but an assessment is not like an ordinary psychotherapeutic session, and, as Josephine Klein (1999) points out, one needs to be clear what one is assessing for: the patient, the institution, oneself, or the treatment we are offering?

As we have tried to make clear in this guide, psychoanlysis and psychoanalytic therapy may not be suitable, appropriate, or necessary for everyone coming for help. But, as Bresnick (1998) said, "Freud's theory and practice of analysing transference has produced a therapy that remains the best method of investigating the proliferating depths of human desire".

REFERENCES

Baker, R. (1980). The finding of "not suitable" in the selection of supervised cases. *International Review of Psycho-Analysis, 7*: 353–364.

Bird, B. (1972). Notes on transference. *Journal of the American Psychoanalytic Association, 20*: 267–301.

Bollas, C. (2000). *Hysteria*. London: Routledge.

Bolognini, S. (2006). The profession of Ferryman. *International Journal of Psycho-Analysis, 87*(1): 25–42.

Bresnick, A. (1998). *The Times Literary Supplement*, 30 October.

Coltart, N. (1988). The assessment of psychological-mindedness in the diagnostic interview. *British Journal of Psychiatry, 153*: 819–820.

Coltart, N. (1993). *How to Survive as a Psychotherapist*. London: Sheldon Press.

Fenichel, O. (1946). *The Psychoanalytic Theory of Neurosis*. London: Routledge and Kegan Paul Ltd.

Fonagy, P., Steele, M., Steele, H., Leigh, T., Kennedy, R., Mattoon, G., & Target, M. (1995). Attachment, the reflective self, and borderline states: the predictive specificity of the Adult Attachment Interview and pathological emotional development. In: S. Goldberg, R. Muir & J. Kerr (Eds.), *Attachment Theory: Social Developmental and Clinical Perspectives*. New York: Analytic Press.

Freud, S. (1904a). Freud's psycho-analytic procedure. *S.E., 7*: 249–256. London: Hogarth.

Freud, S. (1905a). On psychotherapy. *S.E.*, 7: 257–270. London: Hogarth.

Freud, S. (1912b). The dynamics of transference. *S.E.*, 12: 97–108. London: Hogarth.

Freud, S. (1912e). Recommendations to physicians practising psycho-analysis. *S.E.*, 12: 109–120.

Freud, S. (1937c). Analysis terminable and interminable. *S.E.*, 23: 209–254. London: Hogarth.

Garelick, A. (1994). Psychotherapy assessment: theory and practice. *Psychoanalytic Psychotherapy*, 8(2): 101–116.

Greenson, R. R. (1965). The working alliance and the transference neurosis. *Psycho-Analytic Quarterly*, 34: 155–181.

Greenson, R. R. (1967). *The Technique and Practice of Psycho-Analysis*, Vol. 1. London: Hogarth Press.

Greenson, R. R. (1974). Loving, hating and indifference towards the patient. *International Review of Psycho-Analysis*, 1: 259–266.

Greenson, R. R. (1992). *The Technique and Practice of Psycho-Analysis, Vol. 2: A Memorial Volume to Ralph R. Greenson*, A. Sugarman, R. A. Nemiroff, & D. P. Greenson (Eds.). Madison, CT: International Universities Press.

Heimann, P. (1950). On counter-transference. *International Journal of Psycho-Analysis*, 31: 81–84.

Hinshelwood, R. D. (1995). Psychodynamic formulation in assessment for psychoanalytic psychotherapy. In: C. Mace (Ed.), *The Art and Science of Assessment in Psychotherapy* (pp. 155–166). London: Routledge.

Holmes, J. (1995). How I assess for psychoanalytic psychotherapy. In: C. Mace (Ed.), *The Art and Science of Assessment in Psychotherapy* (pp. 27–41). London: Routledge.

Hopper, E. (1991). Encapsulation as a defence against a fear of annihilation. *International Journal of Psycho-Analysis*, 70: 601–624.

Joseph, B. (1985). Transference: the total situation. *International Journal of Psycho-Analysis*, 66: 447–454.

Kächele, H., & Thomä, H. (1987). *Psychoanalytic Practice*. New York: Springer Verlag.

Kernberg, O. (1984). *Severe Personality Disorders*. New Haven/London: Yale University Press.

Klauber, J. (1971). Personal attitudes to psychoanalytic consultation. In: *Difficulties in the Analytic Encounter* (pp. 141–159). New York: Jason Aronson, 1981.

Klauber, J. (1981). *Difficulties in the Analytic Encounter*. New York: Jason Aronson [reprinted London: Karnac, 1986].

Klein, J. (1999). Assessment—what for? Who for? *British Journal of Psychotherapy, 15*(3): 333–345.

Kuiper, P. C. (1968). Indications and contra-indications for psychoanalytic treatment. *International Journal of Psycho-Analysis, 49*: 261–264.

Langs, R. (1982). *Psychotherapy: A Basic Trust.* New York: Jason Aronson.

Limentani, A. (1972). The assessment of analysability: a major hazard in selection for psychoanalysis. *International Journal of Psycho-Analysis, 53*: 352–361.

Limentani, A. (1989). *Between Freud and Klein.* London: Free Association Books.

McDougall, J. (1989). *Theatres of the Body.* London: Free Association Books.

Ogden, T. (1989). *The Primitive Edge of Experience.* London: Karnac.

Quinodoz, D. (2003). *Words That Touch.* London: Karnac.

Rosenfeld, H. A. (1969). The treatment of psychotic states by psychoanalysis: an historical approach. *International Journal of Psycho-Analysis, 50*: 615–631.

Sandler, J., Dare, C., & Holder, A. (1973). *The Patient and the Analyst.* London: Karnac [revised edition 1992].

Schachter, J. (1997). Transference and countertransference dynamics in the assessment process. *Psychoanalytic Psychotherapy, 11*(1): 59–71.

Schubart, W. (1989). The patient in the psychoanalyst's consulting room: the first consultation as a psychoanalytic encounter. *International Journal of Psycho-Analysis, 70*: 423–432.

Shapiro, S. (1984). The initial assessment of the patient: a psychoanalytic approach. *International Review of Psycho-Analysis, 11*: 11–25.

Temperley, J. (1984). Settings for psychotherapy. *British Journal of Psychotherapy, 1*(2): 101–111.

Tonnesmann, M. (1998). Foreword. In: J. Cooper & H. Alfillé (Eds.), *Assessment in Psychotherapy* (pp. ix–xii). London: Karnac.

Tyson, R. L., & Sandler, J. (1971). Problems in the selection of patients for psychoanalysis: comments on the application of the concepts of "indications", "suitability" and "analysability". *British Journal of Medical Psychology, 44*: 211–228.

Waelder, R. (1960). *Basic Theory of Psychoanalysis.* New York: International Universities Press.

Wallerstein, R. S. (1989). Psychoanalysis and psychotherapy: an historical perspective. *International Journal of Psycho-Analysis, 70*: 563–593.

Winnicott, D. W. (1960). Countertransference. *British Journal of Medical Psychology, 33*: 17–21.

Zetzel, E. (1968). The so-called good hysteric. *International Journal of Psycho-Analysis, 49*: 256–260.

Zetzel, E. (1970). *The Capacity for Emotional Growth.* New York: International Universities Press, 1970 [reprinted London: Karnac, 1987].

INDEX

Adult Attachment Interview, 13
affect, 14, 21, 23
alliance, 16, 27, 35
  therapeutic, 8, 15, 21, 24
anger, 23, 42
Anna Freud Centre, 2
anxiety, 1, 6, 14–15, 18–19, 23,
  29–30, 34, 36, 41, 43, 45, 47
  paranoid, 8
  separation, 13
  tolerance, 10, 12
Arbours therapeutic community, 38
assessment, ix–xii, 1–7, 9–10, 13–20,
  23, 25–26, 28–31, 33–38, 41–43,
  47–48
  consultation, x–xi, 2, 7, 9–10,
    19–20, 26, 28–30, 36, 41, 48
  extended, 2
  interview, 19
  psychiatric, 23
  psychotherapeutic, 9

attachment, 5
  infant, 13
  transference, 5

Baker, R., 15, 37, 49
behaviour, 27, 35, 37, 44
  addictive, 22
  obsessional, 7
  risk-taking, 21
  transference, 31
Bird, B., 26, 49
Bollas, C., 11, 49
Bolognini, S., 2, 49
Bresnick, A., 48, 49
British Association of
  Psychotherapists, 24

case studies,
  Mr A, 42
  Mrs L, 42
  Mrs P, 30

Chicago seven, 35
cognitive behaviour, 38
Coltart, N., 7, 13–14, 34, 49
conflict, 2, 6, 13, 20, 23, 27–28,
    35–36, 41–43
  internal, 9, 34
  neurotic, 10
  Oedipal, 7
conscious(ness), x, 4, 8, 20–21, 26, 37
  see also: unconscious(ness)
countertransference, x, 3, 13, 16,
    24–25, 27–31, 34
  see also: transference
  negative, 30–31, 34

Dare, C., 26–27, 51
death, 7, 15, 30, 39, 44–45
  see also: instinct
depression, 11, 33–34, 44, 47
  position, 23
development(al), 7, 10–12, 14, 22,
    |26
  history, 9, 20
  libidinal, 7
  professional, 6
  psychic, 11
  psychosexual, 22
dyad, 7

ego, 4, 7, 15, 19, 27, 38
  auxiliary, 38
  fragile, 12
  healthy, 38
  strength, 10, 12, 14–15, 17, 23
  super, 23
  -syntonic, 11
  weakness, 37
envy, 15

Fenichel, O., 31
Fonagy, P., 13, 49
free association, 13, 22
Freud, S., 4, 6, 10–11, 13, 25–27, 33,
    36, 38, 44, 48–50

Garelick, A., 1, 15, 21, 50
Greenson, R. R., 16–18, 26–27, 29,
    31, 38, 50

Heimann, P., 27, 50
Hinshelwood, R. D., 29, 48, 50
Holder, A., 26–27, 51
Holmes, J., 19, 37, 39, 50
Hopper, E., 33, 50

indication, xi, 6, 9, 15, 23–24, 33–34,
    37, 43
  contra-, x, 22–23, 33–35, 37–39
instinct, 31
  death, 15
  life, 15, 26
introjections, 27

Joseph, B., 21, 50

Kächele, H., 37, 50
Kennedy, R., 13, 49
Kernberg, O., 12, 50
Klauber, J., 19, 36–37, 38, 50
Klein, J., 48, 51
Kleinian, 23, 27
Kuiper, P. C., 37, 51

Langs, R., 35, 51
Leigh, T., 13, 49
life, 2–3, 6, 15, 21, 25–27, 34–37, 39,
    41, 43–44 see also: instinct
  dream, 22
  early, 9
  experience, 9
  external, 38
  family, 3, 22
  history, 29
  inner, 9
  mental, 14
  patient's, 19, 43
  present, 20
  story, 10
Limentani, A., 35, 37, 39, 51

Mattoon, G., 13, 49
McDougall, J., 12, 51
Menninger Foundation, 10
mother, 3, 5, 11–12, 20, 22, 28, 30, 43–44
    bad, 29
    problematic, 29
    single, 20
mourn(ing), 3, 7, 11, 23

narcissism, 1, 6, 11–12, 16, 33
    disorder, 12, 15
National Health Service (NHS), x, 22

object, 12, 15, 20–21, 23, 25–26, 29
    constancy, 12
    good, 3, 29, 35
    part, 12
    primary, 3, 28
    relations, 7, 9, 12, 16, 20, 25, 36–37
    transference, 13, 27
    transitional, 3, 6, 41
objective/objectivity, 9–10, 13–14, 27, 35
Oedipal, 11
    conflicts, 7
    disturbance, 11
Ogden, T., 34, 51

parent(s), 21–23, 28, 36–37, 41
    grand, 3, 21
Portman Clinic, 35
projection, 14, 25, 27
projective identification, 11, 37
psychological mindedness, 7, 14, 23, 34

Quinodoz, D., 4, 13, 20, 51

repression, 25–26, 37, 48
Rosenfeld, H. A., 26, 51

sadism, 15
Sandler, J., 4, 26–27, 34, 51
Schachter, J., 29–30, 51
schizophrenic, 26
Schubart, W., 19, 51
self, 20
    aware(ness), 14, 34
    destructive, 35
    -esteem, 14, 37
    harm, 21
    referral, 6
    understanding, 37
sexual, 21, 36, 43–44
    development, 22
    encounters, 11
Shapiro, S., 25, 51
Solms, M., 34, 39
splitting, 11–12, 18, 29, 35, 37
Steele, H., 13, 49
Steele, M., 13, 49
suicide, 3, 10, 17, 21–22

Target, M., 13, 49
Temperley, J., 5, 51
Thomä, H., 37, 50
Tonnesmann, M., 10, 51
transference, x, 3, 5, 8, 10, 12, 14–15, 18, 24–31, 44, 48 see also: countertransference, object
    attachment, 5
    erotic, 34
    false, 26, 28
    hostile, 30
    negative, 29, 34
    neurosis, 10, 25, 27, 31
    paranoid, 30
    phenomena, 26
    positive, 28
    pseudo-, 26, 28
    psychosis, 26
    regressive, 36
    relationship, 20, 26, 28–30, 33
    unconscious, 21

transferential relationship, 29
Tyson, R. L., 4, 34, 51

unconscious(ness), ix–xi, 1, 3–4,
    6, 11–12, 14–15, 19–20,
    22–23, 26, 28, 31, 37, 48
    see also: conscious(ness),
    transference
phantasies, 9
transference, 21

Waelder, R., 25, 51
Wallerstein, R. S., 10, 51
Winnicott, D. W., 7, 9, 11, 15, 27, 41,
    52
world, 7, 31
    external, 6, 20
    internal, xi, 3–5, 13, 15, 22, 37, 44,
    48

Zetzel, E., 7, 11, 14, 26, 36, 52